Where the Wind Blows

The Underground Edition

Living for Christ in a Hostile World

By
Dorothy Gable

WHERE THE WIND BLOWS
THE UNDERGROUND EDITION:
Living for Christ in a Hostile World

Copyright © 2021 by Dorothy Gable

ISBN: 978-0-9996874-8-2 (sc)
ISBN: 978-0-9996874-9-9 (e)

Title page art: Carol Hartmann
Cover Design by: www/bookcoverdesigner.co

Book 1 — *Where the Wind Blows: The Sound*
Book 2 — *Where the Wind Blows: The Call*
Book 3 — *Where the Wind Blows: The Halls of Faith*
A Christian fiction novel series
of the persecuted faith and God's overcoming

THE UNDERGROUND EDITION:
Living for Christ in a Hostile World
The non-fiction sequel to the *Where the Wind Blows* series

TABLE OF CONTENTS

FOREWORD

"It was the best of times, it was the worst of times, it was the age of wisdom, it was the age of foolishness, it was the epoch of belief, it was the epoch of incredulity, it was the season of Light, it was the season of Darkness, it was the spring of hope, it was the winter of despair... In short, the period was so far like the present period...."

So wrote Charles Dickens in *A Tale of Two Cities* about the conditions during the French Revolution's "Reign of Terror" that took place two and a quarter centuries ago.

History repeats itself.

Whether or not I am personally aware of and/or experiencing reigns of terror in my corner of this sin-infected planet, de-Christianization agendas and programs are present realities around the world. This short book by Dorothy Gable, a trusted friend and gifted writer, prepares us as children of God to face the same reality in our country. In our cities. In our communities.

Dorothy has fittingly chosen to make this small book a part of her *Where the Wind Blows* Biblical Christian Fiction series. But this book is not fiction. It encapsulates the biblical truths that prompted her to write the novels. This is a straightforward, practical handbook *"for such a time as this"* (Esther 4:14), pointing us back to the unshakeable foundation of the proven Word of God and the glorious gospel of Christ. It is written to equip and encourage God's people *"to withstand in the evil day, and having done all, to stand"* (Ephesians 6:13).

———

Whatever lies ahead, I pray the Lord to use this little book to strengthen you to stand with His truth, walk in His love, radiate His joy, and share His gospel of peace—as you pray for the very ones who oppose both you and His Word.

"The people who know their God shall stand firm and take action" (Daniel 11:32).

– Paul D. Bramsen

President, ROCK International

Multi-Media Resource Developer

Introduction
ARE WE READY?

PLUNGING DOWN THE cliff into the abyss—are we ready? I'm not asking if we have enough food laid up with our generators primed and gasoline stored away. I'm not referring to prepping, physically speaking. I am asking myself, "Am I spiritually ready?" And you, "Are you spiritually ready?"

Okay, so what do I have to do? What will it look like? What would be the goalpost? This book goes along with my novel series, *Where the Wind Blows*. The characters had to face these questions and consider if they were willing to reach the world for Christ and stand for Him. However, that series was fiction with a neat ending, and everything made right in the end.

But we are not in heaven yet, and seemingly, the time for judgment, sifting and revealing are at hand. With each coming day, things didn't break our way. Looking for things to return to normal next month, this fall, or next year proved to be wishful thinking.

Has God abandoned us? Are we cast adrift with no hope? How do we keep our eyes on Christ and God's glory while we are in the midst of this world?

What adjustments should we make in our worship, our spiritual disciplines, and our expectations to weather this storm? Remembering, it might last past our lifetime, we cannot know. But our loving, merciful God knows, and He has a plan.

Chapter One
GOD HAS A PLAN

G OD PLAYS THE *long game*—from before time began.

Even as he chose us in him before the foundation of the world (Ephesians 1:4).

God's plan for the ages is laid out in the Bible—beginning with the creation of the universe to its end, followed by the new heaven and new earth (Revelation 21 and 22).

Before time began God created intelligent beings capable of loving Him, but they had to choose to love Him. Knowing the future, God created the angels, including Lucifer. When this great archangel rebelled against God (Isaiah 14:12-15; Ezekiel 28:12-19), he took a third of the angels with him (Revelation 12:3-4).

God created people and gave them the free will to choose to love Him or rebel against Him. Adam and Eve's choice to disobey God placed all mankind and the world under the curse of sin.

However, before time began, God also planned the greatest rescue of all time—to call out a people for Himself who would choose to walk with Him. By sending His Son—the only human *to earn the right to heaven,* God gave each of us the choice of choosing to love God.

Before Christ even came, the faithful were already looking for a Savior, having the faith to believe in God as their redeemer from sin.

but the righteous shall live by his faith (Habakkuk 2:4).

The righteous shall live by faith (Romans 1:17).

God revealed in His Word the Redeemer's people, tribe and lineage. Clues scattered like bread crumbs throughout the books of the Bible described His coming. Some passages portrayed Him as a suffering servant and others as a conquering king. We now know Christ came first to pay the penalty for our sins. He conquered sin and rose from the dead.

The Bible delineates many predictions that have not yet come to pass. Knowing that Christ fulfilled the prophecies for His first coming, we can search the yet unfulfilled passages with confidence that they too will surely happen.

Today our saving faith rests in a Messiah who made atonement for our sins and is seated at the right hand of the Father, waiting until the time for His return to deal with sinners and welcome the believers into His kingdom on earth—what many call the millennium—that will last for one thousand years (Revelation 20).

Only the Father in heaven knows the day or the hour of Christ's return (Matthew 24:36). During the intervening time between Christ's resurrection and His return, He formed the church—the body of believers who have accepted God's free gift of salvation.

During the Last Supper, Christ told His disciples, *"No longer do I call you servants, for the servant does not know what his master is doing; but I have called you friends, for all that I have heard from my Father I have made known to you"* (John 15:15). Our Bible contains God's plan for us.

So, What Are We to Be Doing During These Times?

All authority in heaven and on earth has been given to me. [19]Go therefore and make disciples of all nations, baptizing them in the name of the Father and of the Son and of the Holy Spirit, [20]teaching them to observe all that I have commanded you. And behold, I am with you always, to the end of the age (Matthew 28:18-20).

The primary command of verse 19 is to make disciples as we go about our lives, as we walk by the way, as we go to the marketplace, as we walk with others. Making disciples includes sharing the wonderful gift of salvation and peace with God. Helpless to save ourselves, Christ came from heaven to make the ultimate sacrifice. We simply need to acknowledge our sin and repent—turning from sin to God. Discipleship begins with salvation and reaches beyond this decision into our continued growth in Christ. Being saved is only the beginning of our relationship with God.

Those of us who have taken this step can remember the changes the Holy Spirit wrought within us. Slowly, our eyes were opened to daily sin habits, with periodic glimpses of the kind of people we were. Not left to wallow, the loving God led us to replace bad habits with good ones, taught us to love one another, instilled a thirst and a hunger for greater intimacy with Him and a love of His Word.

How is this possible? The Holy Spirit regenerated us—creating a living spiritual link to God. When we chose to walk with Him, He helped us change from the inside.

Our views about life and sin and people and goals also changed. Before Christ I was not bothered by movies that promoted abortion. After Christ, I helped a ladies' group in my church understand that abortion was murder and not merely a "Catholic issue."

So, if we know Christ and have peace with God (Romans 5:1), and we are still alive, God has a plan for us to help advance His kingdom. It is an amazing, awesome opportunity that He includes us in His plans!

For by grace you have been saved through faith. And this is not your own doing; it is the gift of God, ⁹not a result of works, so that no one may boast. ¹⁰For we are his workmanship, created in Christ Jesus for good works, which God prepared beforehand, that we should walk in them" (Ephesians 2:8-10).

Christ warned:

If you were of the world, the world would love you as its own; but because you are not of the world, but I chose you out of the world, therefore the world hates you (John 15:19).

Christ encouraged:

Blessed are those who are persecuted for righteousness' sake, for theirs is the kingdom of heaven. ¹¹Blessed are you when others revile you and persecute you and utter all kinds of evil against you falsely on my account. ¹²Rejoice and be glad, for your reward is great in heaven, for so they persecuted the prophets who were before you (Matthew 5:10-12).

We can share the love and grace of God that we enjoy with others so that they too may live life with God in their hearts, but it won't be easy. It cost Jesus His life. It cost the apostles their lives, but they gained so much more.

For whoever would save his life will lose it, but whoever loses his life for my sake will find it. ²⁶For what will it profit a man if he gains the whole world and forfeits his soul? Or what shall a man give in return for his soul? (Matthew 16:25-26).

When we asked Christ to save us, we had finally admitted that we were sinners deserving of hell. By accepting the free gift of salvation, we were transferred into God's kingdom of life and light. However, too many of us accepted the benefits of salvation—peace with God, the indwelling Holy Spirit to guide and strengthen us, but did not consider our duties and responsibilities in God's kingdom.

> *But whatever gain I had, I counted as loss for the sake of Christ. [8]Indeed, I count everything as loss because of the surpassing worth of knowing Christ Jesus my Lord. For his sake I have suffered the loss of all things and count them as rubbish, in order that I may gain Christ [9]and be found in him, not having a righteousness of my own that comes from the law, but that which comes through faith in Christ, the righteousness from God that depends on faith—[10]that I may know him and the power of his resurrection* (Philippians 3:7-10).

Are we willing to give all for Christ as He gave all for us? Will we follow where He leads, standing for truth and sharing the glorious gospel of grace? Do we want to be part of God's plan? Andrew Brunson asked himself these questions while imprisoned by the Turkish government. He decided that Christ was worthy of his all.

Questions for Further Thought

1. Think of a time when you were aware that God had used you to help someone find Christ or helped another believer walk in faith. How did this situation encourage you in the Lord?

_____

_____

_____ ∾

2. How do you see yourself being part of God's plan in your current situation?

Sometimes it's easy to think only professional pastors and teachers are serving God. After we returned home from Canada as missionaries, we sometimes struggled to see how God could use us. Now our ministry happens daily as we live life—at work, teaching scuba diving, sharing the faith with a stranger in a store or at the zoo, encouraging other believers.

_____

_____

_____ ∾

Further Resources:

Check out Gregory Koukl's excellent book, *The Story of Reality* or ROCK International's *King of Glory* DVD or illustrated book highlighting God's plan from creation to the new earth. They present a bird's eye view of God's plan through the ages and help us understand where and how we fit in the grand scheme of life.

Chapter Two

CAN WE TRUST HIM?

CAN WE TRUST God? Why even ask this question? Well then, do we live our lives as if we fully trust our Lord and Savior? Do we pray for His will, even if it's not what we prefer?

In theory, in our hopes and dreams, we do. Can we do it in the midst of the messy realities of life—debilitating illness or injury, sudden deaths, job losses or financial setbacks? We all live in this reality, and no matter how careful we might try to be, in the end, the circumstances that we can control are fewer than we often admit. Can we accept God's will, no matter the inconvenience or terrible consequences? Will we stand for truth (which is His truth according to John 17:17) despite the cost? In the middle of the forest, can we remember the mountain heights?

We know courage is acting in spite of, along with, in the presence of fear. Living trust in God happens in the midst of swirling emotions and sometimes related physical symptoms. While we never know for certain how we will react in catastrophic situations, choosing to trust God amid today's setbacks will help us handle harder choices in the future.

For more than ten years my husband, Ralph, and I ministered to the Swampy Cree of northern Manitoba, Canada. The path to God's Lake Narrows and Moose Lake took years and our trusting God each step of the way.

On our first summer missions' trip to see if the call to this ministry was valid, we were sent to Cormorant, Manitoba. Back in the days before widespread credit card use, I tried to discern how much cash we needed to take with us. However, part way through, we began to run low on cash. I shared this shortfall with one of our mentors. Amanda said, "This is when it gets exciting! Now we will see what God will do."

I tried to react positively to her optimistic spirit, but I was still nervous. At the next Bible study in Cormorant, a young man slapped a $100 Canadian bill on the table and said, "This is my tithe, and God told me to give it to you." I saw the answer as clear as day. Yes, I could trust God for our daily needs.

That answer, while it may have seemed small, helped build our trust as we left regular jobs, attended Bible college, and took the plunge to rely on support when we were only at 30 percent of the proposed amount. Unless a couple is willing to trust God for their finances, they often fail to raise their funds or continue to minister in their current field of service.

We first went to God's Lake Narrows, a remote, fly-in village. After eight years at Moose Lake, God told us we were done and sent us back home. Returning to the States was hard, but He was putting us in exactly the right place to minister to our parents. My mother moved in with us after my father died unexpectanly. Over the years, we continued to see God work through our circumstances even when things didn't work out the way we had expected.

The small tests of trusting God through daily life strengthens us for future hardships and obstacles.

The other side of the coin—trusting in family, careers or anything else—will lead to disappointment and disillusionment. In time the children will grow up, move away, and become busy with their own lives. If we live long enough, we will have to leave our jobs behind. Health, abilities, and activities that once occupied our days will erode away over time. If we are living our lives for the temporal, we can become bitter, withdrawn, imprisoned in despair.

However, if we have kept our focus on Christ, rejoicing in the good He brings, and thankful for His gracious provision and merciful bounty, we can say as Paul said:

> Not that I am speaking of being in need, for I have learned in whatever situation I am to be content. *12I know how to be brought low, and I know how to abound. In any and every circumstance, I have learned the secret of facing plenty and hunger, abundance and need. 13I can do all things through him who strengthens me* (Philippians 4:11-13).

As we fix our eyes on Christ, His provision and direction for our lives, we can be overcomers no matter what. Our lives are not products of chance or cruel fate, but threads in God's plan. We can participate with our whole hearts or we can try to run away (remember Jonah?), but God's will, will be done.

Multiple Bible verses proclaim God's faithfulness. One of my favorites is Proverbs 3:5-6:

> Trust in the LORD with all your heart, and do not lean on your own understanding. *6In all your ways acknowledge him, and he will make straight your paths.*

Countless Bible stories illustrate His loving care. We can trust Him for He cares for us.

> Humble yourselves, therefore, under the mighty hand of God so that at the proper time he may exalt you, *7casting all your anxieties*

on him, because he cares for you. [8]Be sober-minded; be watchful. Your adversary the devil prowls around like a roaring lion, seeking someone to devour. [9]Resist him, firm in your faith, knowing that the same kinds of suffering are being experienced by your brotherhood throughout the world. [10]And after you have suffered a little while, the God of all grace, who has called you to his eternal glory in Christ, will himself restore, confirm, strengthen, and establish you. [11]To him be the dominion forever and ever. Amen (I Peter 5:6-11).

It's not about us. It's about God, and He has a trustworthy plan for each one of us. If we can get a hold of what He is calling us to do, we can, through Him, take a stand.

Questions for Further Thought

1. Think of a time where God challenged you to trust Him, the answer, and how your trust was strengthened.

_____

_____

_____ ∽

2. List your favorite Bible verses about trusting Him and His faithfulness. Some of my favorites are included in my personal memory verse list.

_____

_____

_____ ∽

Further Resources

Concordances, reference Bibles, and online Bible study guides such as e-Sword are great resources for finding verses that will help us stand for God. During some of our most difficult times, I filled a notebook with promises from Isaiah. Let us feed on the Word of God (1 Peter 2:2); let His Word be our spiritual nourishment.

Chapter Three

AMBASSADORS FOR CHRIST

Therefore, we are ambassadors for Christ, God making his appeal through us. We implore you on behalf of Christ, be reconciled to God (2 Corinthians 5:20).

ACCORDING TO THE apostle Paul, we are to see ourselves as ambassadors to the world.

An *ambassador* is an envoy sent to a foreign land to carry the official message of the leaders of their home country. Ambassadors are expected to be well informed not only about the communications they bring, but also how to connect with the culture and people. Associating with other leaders requires their being diplomatic, tactful and engaged.

Whose Kingdom Do We Represent?

God's heavenly kingdom. When we were reconciled to God through Jesus Christ, we were new creations (2 Corinthians 5:17) adopted into God's family (John 1:12) and given a heavenly citizenship.

But our citizenship is in heaven, and from it we await a Savior, the Lord Jesus Christ (Philippians 3:20).

He has delivered us from the domain of darkness and transferred us to the kingdom of his beloved Son, ¹⁴in whom we have redemption, the forgiveness of sins (Colossians 1:13-14).

So, while we walk this earth, we are to think of ourselves not only as residents of the countries we now inhabit, but also as heavenly citizens with a guarantee that one day He will take us home.

In him you also, when you heard the word of truth, the gospel of your salvation, and believed in him, were sealed with the promised Holy Spirit, [14]who is the guarantee of our inheritance until we acquire possession of it, to the praise of his glory (Ephesians 1:13-14).

What Is the Message We Carry?

Be reconciled to God—the result of the good news of the gospel. When we surrendered to God and asked Christ to save us, we had peace with God for the first time in our lives. The inner conviction and burden of guilt that we all worked to ignore and covered up, had been cast away *"as far as the east is from the west, so far does he remove our transgressions from us"* (Psalm 103:12). *"I, I am he who blots out your transgressions for my own sake, and I will not remember your sins"* (Isaiah 43:25).

No one is able to save themselves. Only Christ's sacrifice on the cross is sufficient to remove a person's sin. Ephesians 2:8-9 tells us that salvation is not by our own works. God gets the glory and the recognition for our salvation. Everyone is born with a sin nature, and while some seem to do many good deeds, these are never enough to earn their way to heaven.

If it were possible that we could save ourselves, why would God the Father send His Son and place the world's sin upon Jesus? The anticipation was so terrifyingly hideous to the Son of God, who had always been in fellowship with the Father, that the agony of separation on the cross caused Christ to struggle with the sacrifice in the garden of Gethsemane (Matthew 26:38-42; Luke 22:42-44) and cry out on the cross, *"My God, my God, why have you forsaken me?"* (Matthew 27:46).

Yet it was the will of the LORD to crush him; he has put him to grief, when his soul makes an offering for guilt (Isaiah 53:10).

For our sake he made him to be sin who knew no sin, so that in him we might become the righteousness of God (2 Corinthians 5:21).

Christ redeemed us from the curse of the law by becoming a curse for—for it is written, "Cursed is everyone who is hanged on a tree" (Galatian 3:13).

And you, who were dead in your trespasses and the uncircumcision of your flesh, God made alive together with him, having forgiven us all our trespasses, ¹⁴by canceling the record of debt that stood against us with its legal demands. This he set aside, nailing it to the cross (Colossians 2:13-14).

The Lord of glory took on human flesh, knowing the fellowship of the Father and His Holy Spirit. Jesus suffered the same separation from God that someone does who dies in their sins. Jesus bore the full penalty of the sins of all mankind for all time. He did it once.

But as it is, he has appeared once for all at the end of the ages to put away sin by the sacrifice of himself (Hebrews 9:26).

He entered once for all into the holy places, not by means of the blood of goats and calves but by means of his own blood, thus securing an eternal redemption (Hebrews 9:12).

The price was His life; *He was cut off out of the land of the living* (Isaiah 53:8). He suffered what every person deserves to experience. Christ suffered so that we might *"be one, just as you, Father, are in me, and I in you, that they also may be in us, so that the world may believe that you have sent me"* (John 17:21). He lived and died for us so that we could be with God the Father, God the Son and God the Holy Spirit in heaven someday.

Not only that, Jesus' triumph over sin ripped the temple veil blocking the Holy of Holies (Matthew 27:51). He opened the way to God for all who would come by the Son. At the Last Supper, Christ said, *"This cup that is poured out for you is the new covenant in my blood"* (Luke 22:20). Jeremiah prophesied of a future new covenant in verses 31:31-34:

For this is the covenant that I will make with the house of Israel after those days, declares the LORD: I will put my law within them, and I will write it on their hearts. And I will be their God, and they shall be my people (v. 33).

The prophets did not know about the church, which was the mystery that Paul referred to in Ephesians. The new covenant opens the way for all people to be reconciled to God and experience the presence of the Holy Spirit dwelling within them.

You, however, are not in the flesh but in the Spirit, if in fact the

Spirit of God dwells in you. Anyone who does not have the Spirit of Christ does not belong to him (Romans 8:9).

Indwelt by the Holy Spirit, we are commanded (remember Matthew 28:19-20) to share this wonderful news with all whom God brings in our paths. This job of ambassador for Christ is not only for the professional pastor, Bible teacher or professor, but for all believers.

God sends us to different places—where we work, shop, hike, ski, swim, as well as gathering for our various associations and with our friends. He does not call us to be like a turtle, drawing into our shell away from the world and waiting out the bad times until things return to normal. No, God calls us to be *in* the world but not *of* the world.

Do not be conformed to this world, but be transformed by the renewal of your mind, that by testing you may discern what is the will of God, what is good and acceptable and perfect (Romans 12:2).

And in our transformation as citizens of heaven and Christ the King, we are to share this glorious message. In this way we can be ambassadors for Christ and not victims of a hostile and cruel world.

For this reason, Christ tells us to love each other and to love our enemies. For in the world of our past before our salvation, earthly standards determined friend and foe.

But if Christ saved us, He can save that neighbor who insults and swears at us, that co-worker who steals our ideas or gossips about us, and even that criminal. Anyone can be redeemed by Jesus Christ as long as they are alive and breathing.

From society's point of view, some of our friends and neighbors appear to be doing extremely well. They seem to be good, moral people who have it all together. However, God judges people against His holy standard, and against that standard, no one is good enough. Romans 3:23 says, *"for all have sinned and fall short of the glory of God."*

We must share the message with love. We need to be ready to share the gospel with diplomatic tact, consideration and love with everyone every opportunity we have. The Bible calls us to speak the truth in love (Ephesians 4:15).

> *If I speak in the tongues of men and of angels, but have not love, I am a noisy gong or a clanging cymbal. ²And if I have prophetic powers, and understand all mysteries and all knowledge, and if I have all faith, so as to remove mountains, but have not love, I am nothing. ³If I give away all I have, and if I deliver up my body to be burned, but have not love, I gain nothing* (I Corinthians 13:1-3).

What Is the Basic Outline of Our Message of the Gospel?

- We are all sinners; we need a Savior.

- Christ died for our sins and rose from the dead, conquering sin and death.

- Believe on the Lord Jesus Christ, and you will be saved.

Other items or points could be added to these simplified steps, but we need to have a grasp of the depth of the sin of mankind, Christ's ability to save to the uttermost and His desire for us to seek His complete forgiveness.

Let us never forget that this is the most important question: does God *know* you? For anyone to die in his or her sins is a horrifying way to end this earthly life.

On that day many will say to me, "Lord, Lord, did we not proph-
esy in your name, and cast out demons in your name, and do
many mighty works in your name?" 23And then will I declare to
them, "I never knew you; depart from me, you workers of law-
lessness" (Matthew 7:22-23).

If we have been saved for a long time, forgetting how hard life was before Christ is easy. It is easier to consider that our nice neighbor, co-worker or relative is doing okay. Sharing this message is hard; hearing this message is hard, but the Holy Spirit will help us. We don't have to have all the answers or be able to answer every question. However, we do need to make a connection and share our lives of faith.

While at God's Lake Narrows, we worked with a Cree pastor from Garden Hill on Island Lake. He said, "You fish where the fish are. So, you try a spot and see if any bite. If they don't, move on. It is the same with sharing the gospel. Tell them something and see if they are inter-ested or ask to know more. If not, try someone else."

God calls us to be faithful stewards of the gifts and love of God (1 Corinthians 4:1-2), but we must remember that God gives the in-crease; that's His work (1 Corinthians 3:5-9). We are to bring the mes-sage; receiving it is up to those who hear. God opens their hearts to the new life in Christ.

Undergirded, part of, and primary to sharing our faith is covenant-ing with God and other believers in prayer. The great spiritual armor in Ephesians 6 is founded upon prayer.

Praying at all times in the Spirit, with all prayer and supplica-
tion. To that end, keep alert with all perseverance, making sup-
plication for all the saints, 19and also for me, that words may be

given to me in opening my mouth boldly to proclaim the mystery of the gospel, [20]for which I am an ambassador in chains, that I may declare it boldly, as I ought to speak (Ephesians 6:18-20).

Questions for Further Thought

1. Who has God laid on your heart? Who are your prayer partners or supporters?

_____

_____

_____

_____ ⟡

2. Do your own research and develop some key verses for sharing the gospel and memorize them. Remember, no one has all the answers. Saying, "I don't know, but I will find out and get back to you," is perfectly acceptable.

_____

_____

_____

_____ ⟡

3. Discuss ways to connect with people and begin a conversation. One church developed pocket-size prayer cards to record the prayer requests of their neighbors or colleagues.

_____

_____

_____

_____ ⟡

4. Conduct targeted Bible studies about various aspects of the gospel message. For example, what do the verses about hell tell us about the place?

_____

_____

_____

_____

Chapter Four

SHARING THE MESSAGE
WITH THE WORLD

*But in your hearts honor Christ the Lord as holy, always being
prepared to make a defense to anyone who asks you for a reason
for the hope that is in you; yet do it with gentleness and respect*
(1 Peter 3:15).

I PETER 3:15 HAS ALWAYS been one of my favorite memory verses. Throughout the Bible certain verses seem to leap off the page
and out of their context. One such verse to me is 1 Peter 3:15. What is
the context of this verse?

*Do not repay evil for evil or reviling for reviling, but on the con-
trary, bless, for to this you were called, that you may obtain a
blessing. ¹⁰For "Whoever desires to love life and see good days, let
him keep his tongue from evil and his lips from speaking deceit;
¹¹let him turn away from evil and do good; let him seek peace and
pursue it....*

*¹⁴But even if you should suffer for righteousness' sake, you will
be blessed. Have no fear of them, nor be troubled, ¹⁵**but in your
hearts honor Christ the Lord as holy, always being prepared
to make a defense to anyone who asks you for a reason for the
hope that is in you; yet do it with gentleness and respect**, ¹⁶hav-
ing a good conscience, so that, when you are slandered, those*

who revile your good behavior in Christ may be put to shame. *[17]For it is better to suffer for doing good, if that should be God's will, than for doing evil.* *[18]For Christ also suffered once for sins, the righteous for the unrighteous, that he might bring us to God, being put to death in the flesh but made alive in the spirit...*

[4:12]Beloved, do not be surprised at the fiery trial when it comes upon you to test you, as though something strange were happening to you. *[13]But rejoice insofar as you share Christ's sufferings, that you may also rejoice and be glad when his glory is revealed.* *[14]If you are insulted for the name of Christ, you are blessed, because the Spirit of glory and of God rests upon you.* *[15]But let none of you suffer as a murderer or a thief or an evildoer or as a meddler.* *[16]Yet if anyone suffers as a Christian, let him not be ashamed, but let him glorify God in that name* (1 Peter 3:9-18; 4:12-16).

The context of these verses is to respond with love and kindness to intense, physical persecution. In other words, we are not to respond in like kind—anger for anger, name calling with name calling, spite and vengeance with spite and vengeance.

No, beginning with the beatitudes in Matthew chapters 5 through 7 and Luke chapter 6, Jesus laid out the characteristics, the lifestyle, the behaviors of those who want to follow God. After listing the rewards for the humble, sorrowful, seekers of righteousness, pure in heart and peacemakers, Christ proclaimed:

Blessed are those who are persecuted for righteousness' sake, for theirs is the kingdom of heaven. *[11]Blessed are you when others revile you and persecute you and utter all kinds of evil against*

you falsely on my account. ¹²Rejoice and be glad, for your reward
is great in heaven, for so they persecuted the prophets who were
before you (Matthew 5:10-12).

Good conquers evil, and light overcomes darkness. When we
are weak, Christ can be strong through us; the joy of the Lord is our
strength! Does this sound upside down? In Acts 17:6 those oppos-
ing God's work in this world told the magistrates, *"These men who*
have turned the world upside down have come here also." That accu-
sation was the world's viewpoint—living for Christ turns the world
upside down.

However, the truth is, God's bringing His power and glory, step-
ping into history and walking this earth was another step toward right-
ing an upside-down world.

If we are to stand for Christ and represent Him to a world overcome by the Wicked One, we must understand I John 4:4:

Little children, you are from God and have overcome them, for
he who is in you is greater than he who is in the world.

The force of God in and through this physical world is far greater than
all of the combined forces of darkness. Jesus was not overcome. Far
from it! Jesus Christ won!

He disarmed the rulers and authorities and put them to open
shame, by triumphing over them in him (Colossians 2:15).

When Christ died for our sins on the cross and satisfied God's pay-
ment for the sins of mankind, He wrested souls from Satan's grasp.

All who accept the gift of salvation by faith in Christ and His finished work on the cross are now taken from Satan's kingdom and placed into God's. The veil ripped, the earth quaked, souls were resurrected and Christ freed the captives!

> *Therefore it says, "When he ascended on high he led a host of captives, and he gave gifts to men," ⁹(In saying, "He ascended," what does it mean but that he had also descended into the lower regions, the earth? ¹⁰He who descended is the one who also ascended far above all the heavens, that he might fill all things* (Ephesians 4:8-10).

Christ won against the forces of darkness. He came the first time to conquer sin and death.

> *Since therefore the children share in flesh and blood, he himself likewise partook of the same things, that through death he might destroy the one who has the power of death, that is, the devil, ¹⁵and deliver all those who through fear of death were subject to lifelong slavery* (Hebrews 2:14-15).

While in this world, it seems as if the physical is more real than the spiritual. However, the Bible considers the physical world as a shadow and a copy. *"These are a shadow of the things to come, but the substance belongs to Christ"* (Colossians 2:17).

God's ways are greater than the ways of this world. He brought the world into existence with a word (Genesis 1); He will conquer evil with a word:

Then I saw heaven opened, and behold, a white horse! The one sitting on it is called Faithful and True, and in righteousness he judges and makes war. [12]His eyes are like a flame of fire, and on his head are many diadems, and he has a name written that no one knows but himself. [13]He is clothed in a robe dipped in blood, and the name by which he is called is The Word of God. [14]And the armies of heaven, arrayed in fine linen, white and pure, were following him on white horses. [15]From his mouth comes a sharp sword with which to strike down the nations, and he will rule them with a rod of iron. He will tread the winepress of the fury of the wrath of God the Almighty (Revelation 19:11-15).

Many make the mistake of assuming that the suffering Servant of God submitted to death on the cross because He was weak. No! He suffered to save us. He will come again to judge sinners and cast them into hell. Because we have a great and powerful God who is above the forces of darkness, we can step aside and not take our own vengeance.

Beloved, never avenge yourselves, but leave it to the wrath of God, for it is written, "Vengeance is mine, I will repay, says the Lord" (Romans 12:19).

Unless and until we understand that we are engaged in a spiritual war that must be waged with spiritual weapons and that only good can overcome evil, we will not effectively stand for Christ.

The greatest passage on spiritual warfare is found in Ephesians 6.

Finally, be strong in the Lord and in the strength of his might. [11]Put on the whole armor of God, that you may be able to stand against the schemes of the devil. [12]For we do not wrestle against flesh and blood, but against the rulers, against the authorities, against the cosmic powers over this present darkness, against the spiritual forces of evil in the heavenly places. [13]Therefore take up the whole armor of God, that you may be able to withstand in the evil day, and having done all to stand firm (vv. 10-13).

We are not called to take on Satan or his legions. We are called to stand in Christ, covered by the blood of the cross (Revelation 12:11) and under God's protection. Our battle is not with the people the Devil will send to harass and persecute us. No, they are the hostages—the victims, the objects of our attention. We stand against the Devil by standing for God, His truth and His message of the gospel.

Christ died for all. He proved His love for everyone. We carry a message of hope, love, life and a future because of Christ. His is the only message that gives life meaning, as well as provides purpose and direction.

Those of us who have been transported from the kingdom of darkness to light and from death to life have this message. And if we repay evil with good and shower the lost with the love of God, they will be reached. Either they will have no excuse at the final great white throne judgment, or they will be reborn as a brother or sister in Christ.

What Comprises Our Armor and Our Weapons?

Stand therefore, having fastened on the belt of truth, and having put on the breastplate of righteousness, [15]and, as shoes for your feet, having put on the readiness given by the gospel of peace. [16]In all circumstances take up the shield of faith, with which you can *extinguish all the flaming darts of the evil one; ¹⁷and take the helmet of salvation, and the sword of the Spirit, which is the word of God, ¹⁸praying at all times in the Spirit, with all prayer and supplication. To that end, keep alert with all perseverance, making supplication for all the saints* (Ephesians 6:14-18).

Truth, righteousness, the gospel of peace, faith and the knowledge of our salvation are our armor. Our weapon is the Word of God. James tells us to stand up to Satan and He will flee. *"Submit yourselves therefore to God. Resist the devil, and he will flee from you"* (James 4:7). Ephesians 6 tells us to stand against, withstand, stand firm and stand therefore. The great and mighty God invites us to be a part of His grand rescue plan, and He tells us how we can do it—only in Him.

How Do We Do This?

How do we return good, pray for blessing and be thankful for those attacking and harming us? How is this possible? Not by our natural selves.

When we were saved, a part of us was set apart and made holy for God's use. Our spirit was made alive in Christ. However, our sinful flesh still follows after the old ways of sin and death.

But I say, walk by the Spirit, and you will not gratify the desires of the flesh. ¹⁷For the desires of the flesh are against the Spirit, and the desires of the Spirit are against the flesh, for these are opposed to each other, to keep you from doing the things you want to do (Galatians 5:16-17).

We have within us both the old and the new man.

Put to death therefore what is earthly in you: sexual immorality, impurity, passion, evil desire and covetousness, which is idolatry. ⁶On account of these the wrath of God is coming. ⁷In these you too once walked, when you were living in them. ⁸But now you must put them all away: anger, wrath, malice, slander, and obscene talk from your mouth. ⁹Do not lie to one another, seeing that you have put off the old self with its practices ¹⁰and have put on the new self, which is being renewed in knowledge after the image of its creator (Colossians 3:5-10).

The sinful flesh in us wars against our redeemed spirit of life in Christ. God, who allowed mankind to choose to sin against Him, is the true author of freedom. We have the choice every day to walk by the dictates of the flesh or the spirit. Each day we can choose to follow our sinful tendencies or lean on the grace and love of God.

The letters of the New Testament are filled with instruction in how we are to live out this love. For me, the best capsule summary is 1 Corinthians 13.

Love is patient and kind; love does not envy or boast; it is not arrogant ⁵or rude. It does not insist on its own way; it is not irritable or resentful; ⁶it does not rejoice at wrongdoing, but rejoices with the truth. ⁷Love bears all things, believes all things, hopes all things, endures all things (vv. 4-7).

How Do We Put This Passage Into Practice?

By letting God work through us. This is where our weakness becomes God's strength through us.

for the joy of the LORD is your strength (Nehemiah 8:10).

But he said to me, "My grace is sufficient for you, for my power is made perfect in weakness." Therefore I will boast all the more gladly of my weaknesses, so that the power of Christ may rest upon me. [10]For the sake of Christ, then, I am content with weaknesses, insults, hardships, persecutions, and calamities. For when I am weak, then I am strong (2 Corinthians 12:9-10).

So, each day we yield to the Holy Spirit as He directs us to live out God's grace and mercy. As we practice connecting in love with others around us, as we forgive, and as we respond with love and grace instead of retaliation, we are learning how to be ambassadors for Christ.

In this way, the early church turned the world upside down. Today the regions of the world undergoing the harshest persecution are seeing the greatest harvest of souls for Christ. If God is enabling the Christians in these regions to stand for Him, He will also enable us.

Questions for Further Thought

1. Discuss how resorting to returning evil for evil negates our witness and opens us to the Enemy's schemes. Examine the value of living by the principles of Ephesians 6:10-18.

_____

_____

_____

_____

2. Discuss ways we can put Romans 12:9-21 into action.

_____

_____

3. Discuss ways to reach neighbors, co-workers, friends and family.

_____

_____

4. How do we make prayer a part of this process? Develop a prayer list and prayer group.

_____

_____

_____

_____

Chapter Five

WITH LOVE FOR FELLOW BELIEVERS

A new commandment I give to you, that you love one another: just as I have loved you, you also are to love one another. [35]By this all people will know that you are my disciples, if you have love for one another (John 13:34-35).

D O WE LOVE other brothers and sisters in Christ? Do we really love them—not returning slander and gossip with slander and gossip? Are we thankful for the difficult people in our Christian fellowship or our contrary Christian relatives? Does the world see a loving church demonstrating the transforming power of the love of Christ to a community or have our churches been co-opted by this world?

The best place to practice loving others starts in the home and our church. Accepting that another brother or sister in Christ would stab us in the back, talk against us, seek to destroy an initiative or a plan to further the gospel is hard to countenance, but it happens. It happens in Christian institutions, including mission boards and Bible colleges as well as churches.

We are sinners saved by grace. While we have a redeemed spirit, we don't always live as if we do. A pastor, an elder, a deacon, a Bible professor, a dean or the president of a Christian non-profit can also be tempted to yield to the forces of darkness. The solution is the same as for reaching those who do not believe—showering our fiercest opponents in the church with Christ's love—the same love He showered on us and that we can extend to them.

Extending Christ's love begins with being thankful and truly praying for God to bless them. I have been there—shocked and surprised by opposition and malicious slander against us. I prayed for my believing adversaries. I prayed for God to make things right and also prayed for Him to "get" them. My prayer time turned into a vicious cycle that did not bring peace and joy.

Holding tightly to grudges, bitterness and resentment even in the church can be easy. The victory came when I stopped praying for God to get my enemies and instead listed their names, thanking God for them and asking Him to bless them. As if standing beside Christ, I felt His love for them and His longing for them to do right. I began seeking ways to help them, with an eye on casting down any hint of the flesh rising up within me to wish them harm. The situations didn't always right themselves the way I would have liked, but my peace and joy returned.

> *Put on then, as God's chosen ones, holy and beloved, compassionate hearts, kindness, humility, meekness, and patience, [13]bearing with one another and, if one has a complaint against another, forgiving each other; as the Lord has forgiven you, so you also must forgive. [14]And above all these put on love, which binds everything together in perfect harmony. [15]And let the peace of Christ rule in your hearts, to which indeed you were called in one body. And be thankful* (Colossians 3:12-15).

As we are commanded to love our enemies, we are also commanded to love those who believe in Christ. Not letting go and forgiving can lead us to be overcome by bitterness.

Strive for peace with everyone, and for the holiness without which no one will see the Lord. [15]See to it that no one fails to obtain the grace of God; that no root of bitterness springs up and causes trouble, and by it many become defiled (Hebrews 12:14-15).

Not forgiving and not letting go of an offense harms us, affecting how we treat our family, friends, and everyone we meet. Our actions betray us. We don't look saved to the world or our friends and family. Our faith is not attractive or appealing. Our actions hollow out our words of hope and life, rendering them a lie.

For you were called to freedom, brothers. Only do not use your freedom as an opportunity for the flesh, but through love serve one another. [14]For the whole law is fulfilled in one word: "You shall love your neighbor as yourself." [15]But if you bite and devour one another, watch out that you are not consumed by one another (Galatians 5:13-15).

An invaluable Bible study is to look at all the *"one-another"* passages. Jesus demonstrated the kind of care we are to demonstrate to one another when He washed the disciples' feet.

When he had washed their feet and put on his outer garments and resumed his place, he said to them, "Do you understand what I have done to you? [13]You call me Teacher and Lord, and you are right, for so I am. [14]If I then, your Lord and Teacher, have washed your feet, you also ought to wash one another's feet. [15]For I have given you an example, that you also should do just as I have done to you (John 13:12-15).

The description of how we are to live love in 1 Corinthians 13 applies to the body of Christ. Putting off what we should not do must be followed by putting on righteousness. The following is an abbreviated list of the *"one-another"* passages:

Let love be genuine. Abhor what is evil; hold fast to what is good. [10]Love one another with brotherly affection. Outdo one another in showing honor. [11]Do not be slothful in zeal, be fervent in spirit, serve the Lord. [12]Rejoice in hope, be patient in tribulation, be constant in prayer. [13]Contribute to the needs of the saints and seek to show hospitality (Romans 12:9-13).

Owe no one anything, except to love each other, for the one who loves another has fulfilled the law (Romans 13:8).

May the God of endurance and encouragement grant you to live in such harmony with one another, in accord with Christ Jesus, [6]that together you may with one voice glorify the God and Father of our Lord Jesus Christ. [7]Therefore welcome one another as Christ has welcomed you, for the glory of God (Romans 15:5-7).

I therefore, a prisoner for the Lord, urge you to walk in a manner worthy of the calling to which you have been called, [2]with all humility and gentleness, with patience, bearing with one another in love, [3]eager to maintain the unity of the Spirit in the bond of peace (Ephesians 4:1-3).

Let all bitterness and wrath and anger and clamor and slander be put away from you, along with all malice. [32]Be kind to one another, tenderhearted, forgiving one another, as God in Christ forgave you (Ephesians 4:31-32).

Addressing one another in psalms and hymns and spiritual songs, singing and making melody to the Lord with your heart, [20]giving thanks always and for everything to God the Father in the name of our Lord Jesus Christ, [21]submitting to one another out of reverence for Christ (Ephesians 5:19-21).

So if there is any encouragement in Christ, any comfort from love, any participation in the Spirit, any affection and sympathy, [2]complete my joy by being of the same mind, having the same love, being in full accord and of one mind. [3]Do nothing from selfish ambition or conceit, but in humility count others more significant than yourselves (Philippians 2:1-3).

Questions for Further Thought

1. Do a Bible study of the *"one-another"* passages. Consider areas where you need to focus on following these commands.

_____

_____

_____

_____

2. How does the unity of the Spirit in the bond of peace (Ephesians 4:3-6) affect how we interact with other believers? In what way should this passage dictate how we interact with believers who attend other churches?

_____

_____

_____

_____

3. How can my church family better love each other?

_____

_____

_____

_____

Chapter Six

HERE WE STAND

And do not fear those who kill the body but cannot kill the soul. Rather fear him who can destroy both soul and body in hell (Matthew 10:28).

L ET US FEAR God over men. Let us stand for Christ and the truth of the gospel—no matter what.

For a long time, American Christians have lived in a bubble of mild-to-nonexistent persecution. The cost most of us have paid to share the gospel and live for God has been minimal. However, while we know God loves us, there is no guarantee He will allow that situation to remain in our country.

If intense, relentless Christian persecution comes, are we ready? And how does the Bible tell us how to handle it?

Let every person be subject to the governing authorities. For there is no authority except from God, and those that exist have been instituted by God. ²Therefore whoever resists the authorities resists what God has appointed, and those who resist will incur judgment (Romans 13:1-2).

At the time Paul penned this passage under the inspiration of the Holy Spirit, the Roman government had been viciously persecuting Christians. Yet Paul is instructing them to be good citizens—to pay their taxes and follow the laws. Are there exceptions?

So they called them and charged them not to speak or teach at all in the name of Jesus. [19]But Peter and John answered them, "Whether it is right in the sight of God to listen to you rather than to God, you must judge, [20]for we cannot but speak of what we have seen and heard" (Acts 4:18-20).

We know God blessed the apostles' preaching the gospel; the Holy Spirit directed their speech. The Holy Spirit, in answer to prayer after this event, confirmed their actions (Acts 4:23-31).

We are to obey the governing authorities, even when it is inconvenient, or we do not agree with the regulations—until they violate God's higher law.

Jesus commands us to make disciples. This includes spreading the Gospel. We are to share the Word of God. This means we need to have a Bible, read it, seek to understand it, and memorize parts of it.

Many passages in the letters describe activities we should be doing with other believers—holding communion, singing hymns, encouraging and building up one another so we are strengthened to share our faith with the world. However, since the Bible provides only general principles with no detailed instructions for how this should be done, the local fellowship decides when, where and how to gather.

Does God guarantee and should we insist that we have the right to gather for worship in a dedicated building on Sunday? Or Wednesday? Can we always expect to be able to meet in organized churches?

How we respond to these questions will affect our ability to be ambassadors for Christ. While the world naturally takes offense at the gospel, there should be no offense in how we conduct ourselves in speech or manner. We should not be rebellious in other areas such as paying taxes or obeying local laws.

We will have to rely on the Holy Spirit as we chart these unknown waters. Already we have seen the persecution of Christians for the free expression of their faith. For example, the baker who never discriminated against any of his clients found that he could not in good conscience bake a wedding cake for a same-sex marriage. Even though he referred the clients to bakers who would be able to fill the order, he was sued and fined.

Issues arise because our faith is a way of life. A committed Christian understands the principles of our beliefs govern everything we do. Our faith is not a religion that we can relegate to private worship or confine our expressions of faith to within church walls.

If laws are enacted that force us to choose between God and the authorities, we must choose God. So, let us determine ahead of time that we will serve God—no matter the cost. But we will be good citizens and obey all laws that do not violate God's higher laws.

It is good to count the cost ahead of time. Are we willing to give up jobs? Are we willing to risk going to prison for sharing our faith or having a Bible? Are we willing to give our lives for Christ?

Biblical freedom is the freedom to choose to live righteously and to speak the truth in love. Christ said that He came to set people free. Many thought He meant that He would overthrow the Roman government. They were looking for political freedom of this world.

But our freedom rests within our faith, transcending political freedom and reaching beyond to eternity. Having political freedom does not guarantee that a person will use that freedom to do right. Political freedom does not guarantee that a country will choose the life of Christ over the life of sin and death.

We demonstrate our faith by choosing to live for God and speaking the truth in spite of a society that resists the faith.

So Jesus said to the Jews who had believed him, "If you abide in my word, you are truly my disciples, [32]and you will know the truth, and the truth will set you free…[34]Jesus answered them, "Truly, truly, I say to you, everyone who practices sin is a slave to sin. [35]The slave does not remain in the house forever; the son remains forever. [36]So, if the Son sets you free, you will be free indeed (John 8:31-32, 34-36).

The freedom Christ brings sets us free from our bondage to sin.

Many of the promises of the Bible were given to people undergoing intense persecution. We have the Holy Spirit to guide and sustain us. Shortly before Christ went to heaven, He said, *"And behold, I am with you always, to the end of the age"* (Matthew 28:20). Hebrews states, *"for he has said, "I will never leave you nor forsake you." [6]So we can confidently say, "The Lord is my helper; I will not fear; what can man do to me?"* (Hebrews 13:5a-6).

As we seek God's face, learn His ways and follow His leading, let us not forget that He promises to be with us as we are ambassadors for Him. Paul wrote, *"For I consider that the sufferings of this present time are not worth comparing with the glory that is to be revealed to us"* (Romans 8:18).

No, in all these things we are more than conquerors through him who loved us. [38]For I am sure that neither death nor life, nor angels nor rulers, nor things present not things to come, nor powers, [39]nor height nor depth, nor anything else in all creation, will be able to separate us from the love of God in Christ Jesus our Lord (Romans 8:37-39).

How Do We Go On?

Let us ask the Lord to provide us with a mission and calling right where we are—in our local communities, jobs and circle of friends. For our home is our mission field; where we are is where we take our stand for Christ.

What we need to do to stand for Christ is simple, but it is not easy.

- Discover God's plan in the Bible.

- Practice the habits of love, forgiveness, grace and mercy.

- Learn about salvation, practice sharing it along with relevant verses.

- If so led, memorize Scriptures and review them regularly to keep it fresh.

- And rest on God and His Holy Spirit to energize, refresh and encourage.

- Above all, rejoice in God and the hope of His calling!

Recommended Reading

Bramsen, Nate. *What If Jesus Meant What He Said?* Dubuque, Ia.: Emmaus International, 2017.

Bramsen, P. D. *King of Glory: His Kingdom Was Seized But He's Taking It Back.* Greenville, S.C.: ROCK International, 2015. Illustrated book of *King of Glory: The Movie,* produced by ROCK International.

Bramsen, Paul D. *The Story of the King: Kingdom Without End.* Dubuque, Ia.: Emmaus International, 2019. Emmaus Correspondence School Bible study that follows the King of Glory products (illustrated book, DVD, and workbook).

Brunson, Andrew, with Craig Borlase. *God's Hostage: A True Story of Persecution, Imprisonment, and Perseverance.* Grand Rapids: Baker Books, 2019.

Dreher, Rod. *Live Not By Lies: A Manual for Christian Dissidents.* New York: Sentinel: An imprint of Penguin Random House, LLC, 2020.

Fischer, Rob. *The Simplicity of Disciple-Making: And 7 Ways We've Complicated It!* Edgar Springs, Mo.: CreateSpace Independent Publishing Platform, 2018.

Hitchcock, Mark. *The End: A Complete Overview of Bible Prophecy and the End of Days.* Carol Stream, Ill.: Tyndale House Publishers, Inc., 2012.

Hodges, Chris. *The Daniel Dilemma: How to Stand Firm & Love Well in a Culture of Compromise*. Nashville: Nelson Books, 2017.

Koukl, Gregory. *The Story of Reality: How the World Began, How It Ends, and Everything Important that Happens in Between*. Grand Rapids: Zondervan, 2017.

Lutzer, Erwin W. *The Church in Babylon: Heeding the Call to Be a Light in the Darkness*. Chicago: Moody Publishers, 2018.

MacLeod, David J. *The Suffering Servant of the Lord: A Prophecy of Jesus Christ*. Dubuque, Ia.: Emmaus Bible College, 2016.

Metaxas, Eric. *Bonhoeffer: Pastor, Marty, Prophet, Spy: A Righteous Gentile Vs. The Third Reich*. Nashville: Thomas Nelson, 2010.

Pentecost, J. Dwight. *Things to Come: A Study in Biblical Eschatology*. Grand Rapids: Zondervan Publishing House, 1958.

Qureshi, Nabeel. *No God But One: A Former Muslim Investigates the Evidence for Islam & Christianity*. Grand Rapids: Zondervan, 2016.

_____. *Seeking Allah, Finding Jesus: A Devout Muslim Encounters Christianity*. Grand Rapids: Zondervan, 2014.

Routley, Jonathan J. *Eternal Submission: A Biblical and Theological Examination*. Eugene, Ore.: Wipf & Stock, 2019.

Rydelnik, Michael, and Edwin Blum, editors. *The Moody Handbook of Messianic Prophecy: Studies and Expositions of the Messiah in the Old Testament*. Chicago: Moody Publishers, 2019.

Schaeffer, Francis. *The Complete Works of Francis Schaeffer*, 5 Volumes.

Carol Stream, Ill.: Crossway, 1988. (Any of the works of Francis Schaeffer help shed light on the underlying philosophy of our age. Some of his best individual books are: *The God Who Is There, Escape from Reason: A Penetrating Analysis of Trends in Modern Thought,* and *He Is There and He Is Not Silent: Does It Make Sense to Believe in God?*)

ACKNOWLEDGMENTS

2020 AND 2021 have been pivotal years. During this time God compelled me to publish the *Where the Wind Blows* trilogy and this final edition to help us prepare for whatever the Lord brings our way.

Thanks to a loving God who made this possible. Thanks to a more-than-supportive husband. And thanks to a great editor and cover designers.

Knowing that God is greater than all the forces of darkness, may these books be a blessing and an encouragement to all who read them.

Bonus Section

DISCUSSION TOPICS

for the *Where the Wind Blows* Series

Where the Wind Blows — The Sound

1. How did Tom accept that being in the Hannibal maximum security prison was God's will for him? What verses helped him find God's plan for him there?

_____

_____

_____

_____

_____

_____

2. How did forgiveness affect Lieutenant Butch Connors? What pushback did Tom receive from other Christians for forgiving Connors? What verses supported Tom's action?

_____

_____

_____

_____

_____

_____

3.   What is the difference between biblical morality and legality? How did Jesus' command in Matthew 22:21 to give to Caesar what is Caesar's and to God what is God's reveal the heart of following Christ in a hostile world?

_____

_____

_____

_____

_____

_____∾

4.   What shame did Tom bear for being a criminal for Christ? What verses could we use to sustain us when we must bear the cost of standing for Christ?

_____

_____

_____

_____

_____

_____∾

Where the Wind Blows — The Call

1. When Tom learned that new laws had outlawed witnessing, how did he struggle with serving Christ? What did he decide to do? What verses supported his decision?

_____

_____

2. How do we consider when to disobey laws without violating biblical principles? How did some of the churches handle the changes to the tax laws and reporting requirements?

_____

_____

3. How did the witness of many Christians enter into Will Master's turn to God?

_____

_____

4. Why did Tom struggle with fleeing the United States? Could God lead one Christian to stay and another to leave their country? How could God work in both situations?

_____

_____

_____

Where the Wind Blows — The Halls of Faith

1. Why was it important for Christians to treat collaborators lovingly? What verses command us to love fellow believers?

_____

_____

_____

_____

_____

_____

2. Why was it difficult for the church to rebuild? What issues could have hindered Christian fellowship?

_____

_____

_____

_____

_____

3. How did Stella Hutton deal with forgiving Will Masters?

_____

_____

_____

_____

_____

4.   How would praying for the Lord's will bring us peace even if this brings death or loss into our lives? What verses command us to pray for God's will?

_____

_____

_____

_____

_____

_____

Made in the USA
Middletown, DE
15 February 2022